SISTERS ON THE GROUND

BY MAX POSNER

DRAMATISTS
PLAY SERVICE
INC.

SISTERS ON THE GROUND
Copyright © 2018, Max Posner

All Rights Reserved

CAUTION: Professionals and amateurs are hereby warned that performance of SISTERS ON THE GROUND is subject to payment of a royalty. It is fully protected under the copyright laws of the United States of America, and of all countries covered by the International Copyright Union (including the Dominion of Canada and the rest of the British Commonwealth), and of all countries covered by the Pan-American Copyright Convention, the Universal Copyright Convention, the Berne Convention, and of all countries with which the United States has reciprocal copyright relations. All rights, including without limitation professional/amateur stage rights, motion picture, recitation, lecturing, public reading, radio broadcasting, television, video or sound recording, all other forms of mechanical, electronic and digital reproduction, transmission and distribution, such as CD, DVD, the Internet, private and file-sharing networks, information storage and retrieval systems, photocopying, and the rights of translation into foreign languages are strictly reserved. Particular emphasis is placed upon the matter of readings, permission for which must be secured from the Author's agent in writing.

The English language stock and amateur stage performance rights in the United States, its territories, possessions and Canada for SISTERS ON THE GROUND are controlled exclusively by Dramatists Play Service, Inc., 440 Park Avenue South, New York, NY 10016. No professional or nonprofessional performance of the Play may be given without obtaining in advance the written permission of Dramatists Play Service, Inc., and paying the requisite fee.

Inquiries concerning all other rights should be addressed to United Talent Agency, 888 Seventh Avenue, 7th Floor, New York NY 10106. Attn: Rachel Viola.

SPECIAL NOTE
Anyone receiving permission to produce SISTERS ON THE GROUND is required to give credit to the Author as sole and exclusive Author of the Play on the title page of all programs distributed in connection with performances of the Play and in all instances in which the title of the Play appears, including printed or digital materials for advertising, publicizing or otherwise exploiting the Play and/or a production thereof. Please see your production license for font size and typeface requirements.

Be advised that there may be additional credits required in all programs and promotional material. Such language will be listed under the "Additional Billing" section of production licenses. It is the licensee's responsibility to ensure any and all required billing is included in the requisite places, per the terms of the license.

SPECIAL NOTE ON SONGS AND RECORDINGS
Dramatists Play Service, Inc. neither holds the rights to nor grants permission to use any songs or recordings mentioned in the Play. Permission for performances of copyrighted songs, arrangements or recordings mentioned in this Play is not included in our license agreement. The permission of the copyright owner(s) must be obtained for any such use. For any songs and/or recordings mentioned in the Play, other songs, arrangements, or recordings may be substituted provided permission from the copyright owner(s) of such songs, arrangements or recordings is obtained; or songs, arrangements or recordings in the public domain may be substituted.

SISTERS ON THE GROUND was commissioned and originally produced by Playwrights Horizons Theater School (Jean Andzulis, Director), with funds provided by the Leading National Theatres Program, a joint initiative of the Doris Duke Charitable Foundation and the Andrew W. Mellon Foundation. It was directed by Ken Rus Schmoll, the production design was by Eric Southern and Jessica Pabst, the co-scenic design and technical direction was by Frank J. Oliva, the sound design was by Dan Rider, and the stage manager was Carolyn Emery. The cast was as follows:

BETH	Aubrey Elenz
HARRIET	Susannah L. Perkins
BEATRICE	Anne E. Hoeg
HANNAH	Siena D'Addario
BONNIE	Simone Black
ABIGAIL	Sarah Lowe
MARCY	Laurel P. Jones
DENNIS	Colin Barham
NADINE	Megan F. Ermilio
GEORGIA	Gabriel E. Kadian

SISTERS ON THE GROUND was further developed at the Educational Theatre Association's 2017 International Thespian Festival.

THE SISTERS

BETH.	21. The realist. Stoic. The oldest living sister.
HARRIET.	19. The revolutionary. Highly sensitive, chronically ill, brilliantly dictatorial.
BEATRICE.	18. The introvert. Verbally apprehensive, creative.
HANNAH.	17. The conformist. Devout and content.
BONNIE.	16. In great dental pain. Low-maintenance.
ABIGAIL.	15. The romantic. Constantly, irrationally optimistic.

THE OTHERS

MARCY.	18. Sexually precocious. A prankster. Much discussed in town.
DENNIS.	17. Sexually un-precocious. Works at his father's tavern. Harmless.
NADINE.	27. Formerly wealthy and currently sad. Not accustomed to this dirt.
GEORGIA.	19. A stranger running through darkness from darkness.

THE PLACE

A field of dirt with subtle slopes and mounds.
Patches of grass on it. A few rocks. The Northeast.

THE TIME

1825.

/// indicates the passing of time. While these shifts can be quick and subtle, we must feel the night jump forward.

THE SONGS

The songs were written by the playwright and are available as MP3s. They will be distributed in licenses for the play.

A NOTE

For most of the play, Bonnie suffers from major tooth pain. Maybe she says many of her lines with her mouth closed, so we hear the intonation more than the words themselves.

ANOTHER NOTE

This play occurs at night. Varying degrees of nighttime, from twilight to midnight to sunrise. The sun is never out. Except during the weddings, when, for some reason, a golden light swallows all. Our eyes need a moment to adjust to this world and this play; it's darkness, it's stillness, characters who lie down as often as they stand up.

DESIGNERS

The audience should surround the ground on all sides. Or, at least most of them. I would focus on making the ground as detailed and real as possible. The audience should be looking down at it, like the sisters are specimens under a microscope. Don't worry about the night sky—they will conjure the stars with their words and faces.

MAKING THE PLAY

These notes were given to the original cast by director Ken Rus Schmoll. Hopefully they are helpful to future directors.

The sisters are people who haven't communicated much, who don't have language. They have lived under dictatorial house rule. Martha, the oldest, was the sole conciliator, and now she's dead. So the sisters are learning about each other, discovering how to communicate with each other. Philosophizing is new. The sisters don't know how to enjoy leisure time. They don't even recognize it as leisure time. Avoid poetry, don't be oblique. Every moment has to be on-the-ground immediate, with real-life consequences.

Never forget the pull between the *inside* and *outside*. This tension holds the play together.

> *INSIDE* = safety, home, comfort, suffocation, physical abuse, warmth (actual temperature), quiet, the known
>
> *OUTSIDE* = danger, death, discomfort, expansiveness, individuality, solitude, cold, nature, the unknown
>
> *INSIDE* = marriage, bundling, tradition, family, normal life
>
> *OUTSIDE* = aloneness, self-sufficiency, free thought, growth, self, the whole world

When lost, four actions you might play:

> 1. You want to comfort the person you are talking to
> 2. You want to pull the person you're talking to back from the brink of danger
> 3. You want someone to truly know and see you.
> 4. You want to change the course of history.

Whenever sisters report something "Papa says" or "Mama says," think of this as possibly the first time Papa or Mama has spoken directly to them. Normally they would have spoken to and through Martha. The act of reporting what the parents say is not an everyday occurrence, but an Event.

Dennis knows them as the seven (now six) sisters who never speak to him or anyone in the village, who live in a strict household. He discovers them on their own, outside. He is perhaps usually very comfortable talking to people, but has to figure out how to reach them.

Marcy knows what it's like to live under strict rule too.

Nadine is looking for new friends out here in the middle of nowhere. The sisters (Beth and Hannah in particular) are uncomfortable around her not just because she is (or, was) from a higher class, but also because they have been sheltered.

About Georgia: The sisters treat Georgia in a way that they want to be treated by the adults, caregivers, in their lives. In modern terms, they don't want to "become their parents." They want to break the cycle of abuse.

Bundling: *noun, verb,* **bun•dling**
a former Anglo custom of a courting couple
occupying the same bed while fully clothed,
as for privacy and warmth in a house where
an entire family shared one room with a fireplace.

—Dictionary.com

SISTERS ON THE GROUND
PART I

Past sunset.

Six sisters roll a gigantic rock across a field of dirt.
This rock is so heavy, all twelve hands on deck.
With great difficulty, they roll it towards the center.
They stand, take a breath, rest.

They look at a loose rectangle of fresh dirt in the corner.
Martha, their sister, was just buried there.

Their hands return to the rock.
They roll it another four feet, it feels even heavier.
They quit, another breath.

Silence.

They stare at the spot where Martha lies buried underground.
Could it be any further?
They roll again, with oomph; so close.
Finally the rock is on top of Martha's grave.
A makeshift headstone for their sister.

They exhale.

Beth stands stoic before the rock, before her sister.
Abigail, Hannah, Bonnie, and Beatrice follow her lead, showing reverence for poor Martha.

Harriet breaks from sisters.
She lies flat on the ground, face-up, in her dress.
This is a strange and sacrilegious thing to do.
Sisters are alarmed, unsure of how to proceed.
They willfully ignore her.
All but Harriet face the grave.

BETH. Lord she was good.

The quiet of not knowing what to say.

She…

Beat.

BEATRICE. She was.

BETH. She was the… She was the best.
When God made Martha he…

Beth can't think of anything.

HARRIET. *(From ground.)* He what?

BETH. He…

HANNAH. He Broke The Mold.

ABIGAIL. He did.

BETH. *(Relieved to have an end to the sentence.)* He broke the mold!

Beat.

BONNIE. He breaking lots of molds?

HANNAH. God's got technique.

The quiet of imagining God making people out of molds.

BEATRICE. Does seem a little inefficient. Making a mold, making a person, Breaking that mold. Making Another Mold, making Another Person, breaking *that* mold then making *another—*

ABIGAIL. *(Earnestly.)* What's a Mold?

Poor young Abigail. How to explain.

HARRIET. *(From ground.)* God stopped using molds, he wanted people to make themselves. You know how people get made now, right? Beth knows, she's done The Thing!

| HANNAH. | ABIGAIL. | BONNIE. |
| You've done The Thing? | Beth! | You have? |

BETH. I have *Not.*
You know you can't be listening to her!

HARRIET. *(From ground.)* You all know the details of The Thing right? Beatrice does.

>*Sisters look to Beatrice, who looks away.*

Hannah?

HANNAH. Yes.

HARRIET. *(From ground.)* Bonnie?

>*Bonnie nods.*

Abigail? Abigail doesn't! Beth tell her.

>*Abigail turns to Beth. Beth does not know where to start, but opens her mouth to try.*

If Beth won't say how people get made I'll give you a hint. Man has to eat a Raccoon, Woman has to eat a Worm, and they both have to pray to The Devil.

HANNAH. Lord Help!

ABIGAIL. *(To grave.)* Oh Martha you were always there to clarify!

>*Abigail breaks from sisters, walks to Harriet. Standing above her:*

But Harriet. Is heaven a wheel?

>*Sisters, looking at the boulder:*

HANNAH. We'll buy a gravestone when the Corn comes, Mama says.

BEATRICE. The babies got real stones.

HARRIET. *(From ground.)* And they didn't even have names.

BETH. First one had a name—Emily.

BEATRICE. *Ellory.*

HARRIET. *(From ground.)* Mama learned.

BETH. Don't Name A Thing Until It Talks.

>*With some ceremony, they each touch the rock, a last farewell. They begin moving towards their tiny, unseen house.*

BONNIE. Owww

BEATRICE. Bonnie?

BONNIE. My tooth hurts.

> *The sisters are almost offstage.*
> *Except for Harriet, who remains on the ground, looking up, mesmerized.*

BETH. *Harriet.*

HARRIET. *(From ground.)* I'm staying.

> *Beth looks down at her. She is the oldest now.*

BETH. You Can't.

> *Harriet doesn't care.*
> *Abigail, Beatrice, Hannah, Bonnie witness the standoff.*
> *Slowly and curiously, they tread back to the center of the ground.*
> *The scuttle of a critter.*

ABIGAIL. You hear that?

HANNAH. Lord help!

> *Sisters clump frightened above Harriet.*

ABIGAIL. Something's coming!

HANNAH. Let's go indoors!

> *The rattle of more critters.*

ABIGAIL. You hear *that*?

HARRIET. *(From ground.)* Sssshhh.

> *At once, all five drop onto the dirty ground, joining Harriet.*
> *This is new and miraculous.*
> *They're looking at the stars.*

HANNAH. Lord *Wow*.

HARRIET. I *know*.

HANNAH. Whoa.

BETH. Oh My Wow.

BONNIE. *(Holding the side of her jaw.)* Ow.

Dennis, a small adolescent, carries an enormous barrel across the field.
Sisters clench, terrified.
He notices them on the ground.
Then, he notices Martha's burial site, puts it together.

DENNIS. She Was Good.

Sisters ignore him, frozen.
He exits.

/ / /

Night has blackened, they are still outside.
Sisters sing a hymn as they drift to sleep under the stars.
By the final verse, all but Harriet are sleeping.

Oh Abraham

BETH, HARRIET, BEATRICE, BONNIE, HANNAH, ABIGAIL.
Oh Abraham
Do you need help
Do you need time
Can I ask you

Oh Abraham
Am I off pitch
Are you upstairs
Am I outside

I have to tell you my dream
I was entirely green
There were eight children
Green green green
I had no clue what to do

Oh Abraham
Can you make sense
Of all my dreams
I need your help

Oh Abraham
Butter is my work

Stitching is nonstop
Winter I am cold

I have to tell you my dream
I was entirely green
There were eight children
Green green green
I had no clue what to do

> *Only Harriet now.*

HARRIET.
That's My Dream
Fright'ning Dream
Oh Abraham
Oh Abraham
Oh Abraham

> * / / /*

> *The next dusk, brighter than before.*
> *Beth stands before sisters, who kneel.*

BETH. Mama still ain't talking but Papa confirmed it. I'm going to marry James.

> *This is strange and large news.*

ABIGAIL. Do you love him?

BETH. Marriage is when love *starts* Abigail.

BEATRICE. But Martha was going to marry James.

BONNIE. (May She Be Content)

HANNAH. Well Beth that's. That's neat! James is—

BONNIE. Yeah!

ABIGAIL. Are you excited?

BETH. I... Yes... Yeah... I mean... Sure... James is......

> *Beth can't think of anything.*

ABIGAIL. He's got...pink cheeks!

BONNIE. That's true.

BEATRICE. He laughs too loud.

HANNAH. Doesn't hear his own voice well.

BETH. He does speak at the wrong volume but…I don't know, I don't think people are very *different* from each other like… When you think of the amount of people popping out every day, having two eyes and a nose and the. I just think people are more similar than. I just think it's.

> *Harriet begins coughing uncontrollably, writhing subtly.*

We should go in.

HARRIET. *(No longer coughing.)* No.

> *A spooky sound—the wind, or a predator.*

BEATRICE. You hear that???

HARRIET. Ssshhh.

> *Sisters lie down, the lights brighten, slightly.*

/ / /

> *The next dusk, earlier than last.*
> *Sisters sit cross-legged in a circle, eyes on Beth.*
> *Harriet lies apart.*

BETH. James confirmed it!

BONNIE.	HANNAH.	ABIGAIL.
Wow!	*Beth!*	Yes!

BETH. So yes. We Will Have A *Horse*!

BONNIE.	HANNAH.	ABIGAIL.
Wow!	Beth!	*Yes!*

BETH. And not just for farming, for fun too—

BONNIE.	HANNAH.	ABIGAIL.
Wow!	Beth!	Yes!

BETH. For travel—

BONNIE.	HANNAH.	ABIGAIL.
Wow!	*Beth!*	Yes!

BETH. So that will be nice.

HARRIET. *(From across the dirt.)* Be very careful Beth.

BETH. I know how to ride.

HARRIET. *(A code.)* Just. Keep in mind what happened to our sister. *Louisa.*

Harriet joins the sister circle.

You remember Louisa, Beatrice?

BEATRICE. May She Be Content.

ABIGAIL.	HANNAH.
Louisa?	Who's Louisa?

HARRIET. *(To Abigail.)* You weren't born yet.

BONNIE.	HANNAH.
Was I?	Was I?

HARRIET. I think they're ready to know. Now that we're outside we can be open about the—

BEATRICE. 'Bout the dark dark—

HARRIET. 'Bout how Martha wasn't the first sister to Go Away. Beth? You think they're old enough?

BETH. *(Solemn.)* Yes.

HARRIET. Louisa our eldest sister May She Be Content was on our horse—

ABIGAIL.	BONNIE.	HANNAH.
She died?	When?	We had a horse?

HARRIET. Louisa was on Our Horse—

BETH. (may she be content)

BEATRICE. Oh I loved that horse!

BETH. Lightning—

HARRIET. And Lightning wasn't just any horse. Lightning had lived for—

BETH. Five hundred years—

BEATRICE. Lightning had lived in Japan—

HARRIET. Japan?

BEATRICE. Yeah Japan.

HARRIET. Beatrice that's…

BEATRICE. What?

BETH. And Out West—

HARRIET. Yeah a British man rode her in the Revolution—

BETH. Died Ontoppa Her.

ABIGAIL.	HANNAH.
No!	Really?

HARRIET. Had those red stains on her white hair from that British man dying on her.

BEATRICE. And then she went to France—

HARRIET. Cuz Lightning wasn't on *anyone's* side.

HANNAH. There's a sister we don't know about?

BEATRICE. Sweet Old Louisa May She Be Content.

HARRIET. And one day Louisa was riding Lightning—

BETH. Picking corn and riding around—

HARRIET. And Lightning started galloping into the woods.

BETH. It's true.

HARRIET. And Louisa screamed "GET ME OFF GET ME OFF GET ME OFF"—

BETH. But that horse was going faster / than

BEATRICE. Than Anything.

ABIGAIL.	HANNAH.
No!	Oh no!

BEATRICE. Papa got the rifle—

ABIGAIL.	HANNAH.
No!	*No!*

HARRIET. Shot at Lightning—

BETH. But Lightning would not die, just galloped faster—

HARRIET. Bulletproof—

BEATRICE. Galloping.

BETH. Papa kept shooting…

HARRIET. And I was the only one who saw this part… You both were sobbing your eyes were too foggy…

BEATRICE and BETH. Lord Help.

HARRIET. But I Saw Papa Shoot Louisa's Leg Off.

HANNAH.	ABIGAIL.	BONNIE.
What!	No!	Really?

HARRIET. 'Til her leg was just like. It was just like.

BETH. Harriet.

HARRIET. You were crying too hard to notice but. That leg was in five parts and I think this story explains Papa. When you think he's being simple he's thinking 'bout that leg.

Beat. Maybe this does explain Papa.

BEATRICE. And THEN we gotta letter from Louisa—

HARRIET. Right.

BEATRICE. And I opened it and I read it. Left to Right and it said: "Dear Sisters: I am with the Indians now."

ABIGAIL.	HANNAH.	BONNIE.
Wow!	My Word.	*Huh.*

HARRIET. (She married a Chief)

BEATRICE. "And I'm So Much Happier Than I ever was with Mama and Papa. The food tastes better. I sleep on the earth—"

HARRIET. "I brought a dead owl back to life this morning."

BEATRICE. And at the end of the letter it said: "The Indians don't hit their children."

HARRIET. *"The Indians don't hit anyone."*

The quiet of recalculating everything.

ABIGAIL. *(To Beatrice.)* You know how to read?

Beth, Beatrice, and Harriet burst out laughing.

BETH. You girls need to start recognizing storytelling.

Beat.

Anyways. Real excited to have a horse soon.

The night darkens.

/ / /

Sisters on the ground. Asleep. In her usual insomnia, Harriet sings.

Saddle

HARRIET.
Saddle below me
Reins in my hand
Hooves on the hilltop
Rocks on the land
Galloping onward
Trotting to sky
Why why why!
Oh tell me now—
Why why why!

The quiet of being unable to sleep.

Is anyone awake?

A long pause, no movement.

Are all of you asleep?

Stillness.

Is anyone awake?

BETH. I am.

HARRIET. Beth. My body's shutting down.

BETH. That only happens Once in your life. Breathe through your nostrils count stars.

HARRIET. I have what Martha had and the thing that's nagging at me is No One Really Knows Me.

BETH. I know you.

HARRIET. What am I then?

BETH. My sister.

HARRIET. But what am I *like*?

BETH. You're like. Wanting attention. Thinking you're sick. Good with a needle.

HARRIET. But what was I *for*?
Was I *for* the needle?

Pause.

BETH. You were for us.

HARRIET. But where does that Go?

BETH. Nowhere?

HARRIET. I'm just having some questions.

BETH. What do you want me to say?

HARRIET. Something permanent.

Harriet is lying near Martha's grave.

Did we know Martha?

BETH. Yes.

HARRIET. Just the outside.

BETH. Harriet.

HARRIET. Not the innercenter… This is why I wish I could write words down!

BETH. You sound drunk.

HARRIET. Wish I was… 'member when they amputated the guy's legs?

BETH. Neighbor Henry?

HARRIET. Whiskey helped.

BETH. You'll wake the others.

Abigail sleep-talking.

ABIGAIL. I think someday it'd be nice if there was a way to just.

Make one part of the body numb. So you could cut it off or fix it up without feeling anything.

Harriet and Beth look at her, confused.

HARRIET. *Yeah.*

Abigail continues sleeping.

BETH. You're *not* dying.

HARRIET. But you're marrying.

BETH. But I'm not *dying.*

HARRIET. But you'll be *far.*

BETH. We can write.

HARRIET. No, We *Can't.*

BETH. *I know.* But. One thing I know about you: you're dramatic.

HARRIET. I'm Dying Of Cholera And Nobody Knows Me.

HANNAH. *(Eyes closed.)* Do The Lord A Favor And Be Silent.

BONNIE. *(Eyes closed.)* We're trying to sleep.

HARRIET. GoodBYE Sisters.

HANNAH. *(Eyes closed.)* Good*night* Harriet.

HARRIET. I saw James eat a spider once he didn't think anyone was noticing. He eats spiders All The Time.

Night blackens.

/ / /

Marcy strolls through, very pregnant, lantern in hand, humming.
She notices six sleeping sisters.
She keeps walking.

/ / /

The deep of night. Half the sisters sleep, but not Bonnie, whose head rotates, scanning the ground.

ABIGAIL. How's your tooth Bonnie?

BONNIE. I don't wanna talk about it… I'm thinking about Walls.

ABIGAIL. Walls?

BONNIE. Just had an idea, I don't know. That maybe you don't need walls. That maybe you don't need walls this time of year.

Abigail almost knows what Bonnie means.

BETH. James is about as good as anyone. Has the same amount of fingers, so—

BONNIE. Ten?

BETH. Yeah ten, so.

Harriet explodes into a coughing fit. Silence.

/ / /

Later. Bonnie crawls, searching for something.
She finds a rock, about the size of a quarter. She puts it in her mouth, looks at her sleeping sisters.
CRUNCH. She eats the rock. Sweeet relief. She lies down to sleep.

/ / /

Later. Sound of a predator, a yelp.
Sisters jolt to standing, alarmed.

ABIGAIL. You hear that?

HANNAH. No.

BEATRICE. I did!

HARRIET. It's a tiger!

HANNAH. No tigers here God Bless.

They huddle.

HARRIET. Keep in mind. They're more scared of you than you are of them.

BEATRICE. You don't know that.

HARRIET. They're always naked so. Imagine how unsafe that would feel so…Think about it.

They think about it. They hold each other tight. They plop

> *down, in unison, spooning. Six spoons.*

/ / /

> *Dawn.*
> *Beatrice waking, sisters still spooning, asleep*

BEATRICE. *(Private.)* I *can* read.

> *She sits, looking at dirt with a reading face.*

HARRIET. *(From spooning.)* Beatrice write this down I've got it! Are you awake? Beatrice! Write this down I've got it.

BEATRICE. I'm reading. It's different than writing.

HARRIET. Mm.

BEATRICE. It's my favorite thing just sitting in a room all alone just reading.

HARRIET. You've never been in a room all alone.

BEATRICE. Ssshhh.

HARRIET. You don't have a book!

> *This is true. Beatrice lies back down.*

/ / /

> *Still dawn. Dennis enters, no barrel, stares at the clump of spooning sisters. He clears his throat. They tense.*

BEATRICE. Who's there?	BONNIE. Hello?
HANNAH. My God.	ABIGAIL. You hear that?

DENNIS. I'm here.

> *The quiet of not knowing who he is.*

Dennis. Your friend Dennis… Not in a bad way I'm just here.

BEATRICE. Dennis?

DENNIS. Yes.

HARRIET. Leave us alone.

BONNIE. You're not our friend.

HANNAH. We just live six houses away from you.

DENNIS. Just wanted to say. I'm sorry for your loss and congratulations on getting married Beth.

> *They don't respond.*

You're going to get dirt on your skirts…
Walking back from The Tavern.
Went my own way because tired of the same voices saying the same drunk things.
Swine Swine Swine Democratic Pigs Wife Wife Swine Big Barn…
Tired of waiting for a wedding or a funeral or the corn to come to talk to you.

BEATRICE. What's in your bag?

DENNIS. A book.

BEATRICE. Give it to me.

HARRIET. Give it to her.

> *He does, immediately.*

DENNIS. …
Can I lie down?

HARRIET. You got a dress?

> *He doesn't.*
> *He exits.*

ABIGAIL. *(Sitting up slightly.)* I never know if he wants to talk to You, You, You, You, You, or Me

HANNAH. Or just Us.

BETH. It does feel a little.

ABIGAIL. Yeah.

BONNIE. A little.

BEATRICE. Unspecific.

/ / /

> *The following sunset. Harriet is on the ground.*

The rest are breathing heavily, having just sprinted from somewhere.

BETH. Marcy gave birth!

HARRIET. Oh Hell Hell Hell, When??

| HANNAH. | ABIGAIL. | BONNIE. |
| You missed it! | Today. | *Oh* Wow. |

HARRIET. Of all the births to miss I had to miss *Marcy's*!

HANNAH. S'what you get for bein' "sick."

BETH. Oh My Wow my stomach is—

BONNIE. Mine too.

ABIGAIL. Wow.

BETH. That was—

BEATRICE. Dear Lord.

HARRIET. What happened tell me everything!

BEATRICE. You want the long one or the short one?

HARRIET. The long one!

BETH. Okay so. It's almost sundown the butter is done and Marcy's going into Labor. We can hear her. So we run over to her house—

BEATRICE. And Marcy still won't say Who It Was. And Midwife's asking her: *"Who Was It?"*

BETH. Her mom, too: *"Who Is He?"*

HANNAH. She says "It Was God"!

BEATRICE. Then she says it was Thomas Jefferson.

HARRIET. No!

BONNIE. Yes.

BETH. *Then* she makes up names.

HARRIET. What?!

BEATRICE. British ones.

HANNAH. Lord ChamberPot.

BETH. Indian ones.

BEATRICE. Chief WaterPuppy.

Gasp.

HANNAH. Lord Help!

BETH. We're crowded round in Marcy's house.

BONNIE. (I officially *do not* like houses by the way)

BETH. Dozen girls dozen women babies. Marcy's Mama's there, white as a ghost. *Mama's* there, never misses a birth.

BEATRICE. Marcy's Mama says to Mama: "You have twelve daughters, they don't break *one* commandment, I have one daughter, she breaks *all* of 'em."

HANNAH. And Mama looks at her and says: "I only have twelve daughters if you count the dead ones."

HARRIET. Mama talked?

BEATRICE. Looked real discomfortable.

BONNIE. Bringing up death at a birth like that?

HARRIET. Then what?

BETH. Marcy's looking at everything like it's all a mistake. And Midwife Wendy's shouting at her: "You *Know* You're Gonna Tell Us *Who He Is*... Was it Jimmy Fisher?"

BEATRICE. "No it was *God*"

BETH. "Was it Samson Conrad?"

BEATRICE. "It was G-O-D"

BETH. And Marcy's screaming and weeping—

ABIGAIL. Loudest sound I ever heard.

BETH. Louder than Rebecca louder than Elizabeth—

BONNIE. Louder than Samantha—

BEATRICE. Louder than Denise—

ABIGAIL. Louder than Lillian—

BONNIE. Louder than Wendy—

BEATRICE. Louder than Annabel—

HANNAH. Louder than Rebecca—

HARRIET. She already said Rebecca, Hannah.

    Beat.

BETH. Marcy's dying in pain there's so much liquid.

HANNAH. Then they make her stand.

ABIGAIL. *(Stands.)* Like this.

BEATRICE. The baby got twisted so they're pressing on her stomach hard. She's standing and like…

ABIGAIL. *(Bouncing.)* Bouncing.

BETH. Births make me tired.

HANNAH. God was punishing.

BETH. But as that littlebaby starts to pop Midwife says sharp: "WHO WAS IT??"

BEATRICE. And you *know* you can't lie through *that* kinda pain…

BETH. And Marcy blurts out…………"Francis Moncrieff!"

HARRIET. No!

HANNAH.	ABIGAIL.	BONNIE.
Yes!	*Francis Moncrieff.*	Yes.

HARRIET. Preacher's Scary Drunk Son?

HANNAH. Lord Wow.

BEATRICE. It's true.

BETH. Baby's out.

ABIGAIL. Blood everywhere.

BONNIE. Baby's shrieking.

BETH. Marcy's crying.

ABIGAIL. Crying cuz the baby's so perfect.

BETH. Crying cuz she *spilled her secret*!

HANNAH. And Mama's running to grab Francis—

BEATRICE. Mama and Stephanie Doober drag him to the house, his face is purple!

HANNAH. Thirty of us waiting for him and—

BETH. He sees Marcy... Sees his baby. They don't say nothing. But Preacher comes in looking Mad like The Queen of England...

BEATRICE. (Preacher's wife already there)

HANNAH. (Melinda)

HARRIET. (I hate Melinda her ma was a Raccoon)

BETH. Preacher doesn't look at drunk son Francis. But he does look at his New Grandson.

BEATRICE. And Francis says: "Sorry Dad."
And Preacher says: "At least you *added* something to the world."
And Preacher swallows, takes a breath, and launches right into *a wedding*!

BETH. And Francis and Marcy Get Married. Right there.

> *Beat.*

HARRIET. *Francis* and *Marcy*. They don't make logic together.

ABIGAIL. They did the thing.

BEATRICE. Don't need to make logic to do the thing.

HANNAH. Don't do the thing with someone you don't make logic with, is the lesson.

> *Beat.*

BETH. *(Confessing.)* I did the thing with someone I don't make logic with.

HANNAH.		HARRIET.
So it's true.	ABIGAIL.	I *told* you.
...	What's The Thing?	
Lord Wow.		

BETH. In a cornfield. Large time ago.

HANNAH. Are you doomed for hell?

BETH. We interrupted.

> *The night has darkened.*

Seeing Marcy and Francis and that Baby got me thinking. Got me

28

thanking God I get to marry James. We make more logic than them, God Bless.

A booming voice, authoritative:

MARCY. What On EARTH Are You Girls Doing Out Here? You're asking to be Slaughtered. GET BACK INSIDE.

Sisters fling onto the ground, like soldiers in battle ducking into a ditch, their bodies make a six-pronged star.

You can't keep sleeping on dirt like a buncha Indians… Can you see who this is?

They can't.

It's Melinda. Preacher's wife and my mom was *not* a Raccoon.
And Beth? Don't talk like *you're* so proper. A cornfield I am shocked!
Thought you were proper wow. You've broken God's trust and he ain't forgetting.
…
We've been hearing your voices out here yakking. For the Good of God Can You Go Indoors!

HARRIET. Our sister died…

MARCY. I know but—

HARRIET. Martha.

ABIGAIL. (Be *quiet* Harriet)

HANNAH. *(Sucking up.)* Preacher did a nice job on her funeral you can tell him that—

MARCY. I will.

HARRIET. Hard to describe her she was so silent.

BETH. Said her name right.

ABIGAIL. Lots of dogs in the chapel.

MARCY. Lotsa dogs yeah—

ABIGAIL. We wanted to just—

BEATRICE. Be alone for a moment—

MARCY. Well I'm sorry 'bout your sister but. You're not alone. You're with Satan.

HARRIET. Not everyone gets four rooms like you and Preacher!

BONNIE. (Don't argue Harriet)

MARCY. Don't have *four* rooms!

HARRIET. You have five!

HANNAH. (Don't *Argue*)

HARRIET. We have one! We hear Mama and Papa doing the—

BONNIE. *I* don't—

HARRIET. I heard them *make* you.

HANNAH and ABIGAIL. Lord Help.

MARCY. Harriet Jackson you stand up right now. I Am Going To Strike You.

    Beat.

Satan has entered this this this. Spot…and there's ample room in your house I've been in your house I stitch with your Ma and… And Beth I'm telling Preacher you're tarnished, and he's telling James. Good luck getting married now nope.

    Marcy bursts out laughing, comes towards them.

I'm not preacher's wife HaHaHAHA!
It's Marcy!

HANNAH. The Devil!

MARCY. *(Concerned.)* I sound like her?

HANNAH. That's your mother-in-law now.

MARCY. I know.

BEATRICE. Marcy do you want to lie out with us?

    They're facing the sky, it's so great.

MARCY. I shouldn't. I should get home to. To my Francis. To my husband. Francis. And. Our baby and. I'll get dirt on my dress.

HARRIET. Dirt and dresses is normal.

HANNAH. Dresses are for washing.

> *Marcy goes for it.*
> *It takes a bit to get down, she did give birth today.*
> *Her head leans back on the dirt, and IMMEDIATELY jolts back up.*
> *The night sky is too intense.*

MARCY. That was nice. To see the sky like that, from like. That angle.
I should walk home now it's been a large day.
…
I like my baby… It'll be okay.
…
I used to sleep with lots of people breathing on me. Brothers mostly, but we were all the same at night. And then they got married or they—

ABIGAIL. May They Be Content.

MARCY. Amen.
…
So, I guess now it's. People breathing on me again. So that's. That's. That's. Good night.

> *Marcy exits.*

/ / /

> *Deep night. Sisters on the ground.*

HARRIET. Is anyone awake?

ABIGAIL. I am.

HARRIET. Don't tell Beth this but James eats spiders Everyday.

BETH. She's tryin' to make me sad I'm getting married.

HARRIET. You are sad.

BETH. I said I don't feel *excited*, that's different than sad.

> *Beat.*

I just haven't been Near him.

> *Beat.*

And now I'll always be Near him. And I like being Not Near things I like being sort of far from things sort of as far as possible from things.

HANNAH. But being near things is so fun.

BEATRICE. I want to choose when I'm near things and when I'm not.

ABIGAIL. I want to always be near Anything.

BETH. I want to choose
…
Being out here wow. I better go inside. Tomorrow is a large day.

HARRIET. How you gonna walk back in the dark?

BETH. Forty steps to the little tree, twenty steps to the funny shrub, eighty steps to the stump, twelve steps to the door.

HARRIET. Papa's sleeping. Drunk as a chipmunk. If we're back by sunrise he ain't noticing.

BETH. But Mama—

HARRIET. Mama ain't talking.

BEATRICE. It's true.

BETH. I just. I gotta practice going.

>   *Harriet starts breathing very heavily. It seems like she is having a major episode, the worst we've seen so far. She's hyperventilating, twitching, spasming. It is very extreme yet somehow plausible.*

HANNAH. Oh no!

ABIGAIL. She's—

BETH. I have to go Harriet I gotta be alone I gotta clear my head I gotta get excited—

BEATRICE. She's gotta go!

BETH. Excited. I'm excited! I'm excited to marry James. He's got ten fingers. He's kind. He's very… I'm excited.

HARRIET. *(Grabbing Beth's torso.)* I
Feel

So
Lucky
To Have Known You All—

BETH. She's not dying.

HARRIET. I see a green light!

BETH. *White* light. That light is White.

HANNAH. Oh Harriet!

> *Harriet stumble-crawls to each sister, saying farewell.*

HARRIET. Oh Hannah!
Oh Bonnie!
Oh Beatrice!
Oh ABIGAIL!
Oh Beth! Enjoy the space. A lot more space. Just you and your *SpiderEater*.

BETH. I'm going, Harriet.

HANNAH. Lord Help!

HARRIET. I'll see you in The Great Wheel of Heaven!

ABIGAIL. *How is it a wheel??*

> *Beth leaves. Harriet grabs her feet, Beth struggles to free herself.*

BEATRICE. She's *Got* To, Harriet

> *Beatrice fights to free Beth's ankles.*

HANNAH. Oh Harriet!

BONNIE. Lord Help!

BETH. And once I'm gone you gotta go back inside! Be like people again!

> *Harriet's body curls over Beth's feet.*
> *Bonnie, Beatrice, Abigail, and Hannah physically move Harriet.*
> *They drop her on the dirt, far from Beth.*
> *Beth moves away.*

HARRIET. Good
Bye
My
Sisters
Be
Ware
Of
Fire.

> *Harriet "dies."*
> *Beth is gone.*

/ / /

> *Golden daylight:*
> *Harriet on the ground, "dead."*
> *Bonnie, Beatrice, Hannah, and Abigail sing the wedding song.*
> *At the end of the song, they place a veil on Beth's head.*

Wedding Song

BONNIE, BEATRICE, HANNAH, and ABIGAIL.
This is a wedding song
It will help you prepare
For your marriage
Which your dad is
Meeting about
Right this instant
He's agreeing
He's assessing
The boy with the plow
The shaky one
The shifty one
The tired one
This is a wedding song
Here's what you do:

Sing me until you're married
Do not stop singing me
Until you're married

Sing me
All the time
Sing me
In your sleep
Sing me
Afternoons
When the
Children Pee
on the
school when the
Boys get
Beaten by
The head
Master and
Birds get
Tired in the
Air oh

You must not stop singing
Until you're married

Sing me
All the time
Sing me
In the barn
Sing me
Undercovers
Sing me
To yourself
When the
Wolves are out
When the
Horses die
When the
Hunger comes
When the
Corn flowers
Yes please

Do not stop singing me
Until you're married

You will be married today
You will be married today
You will be free to stop
Singing
Tomorrow
Stop
Singing
Tomorrow

> *Sisters exit.*

/ / /

Beth's Wedding

> *Nadine, in a very fancy dress, approaches Beth, who sits on Martha's rock. Nadine holds a glistening chamber pot. She presents it to Beth.*

BETH. Thank you Nadine.

NADINE. It's nothing.

BETH. No it's beautiful.

NADINE. You know at my wedding someone gave me a—

BETH. Wow—

NADINE. And I thought—

BETH. No I love it.

NADINE. I thought Gross—

BETH. No—

NADINE. But it really is the wedding gift I use most of all.

BETH. Thank you.

NADINE. It's small.

BETH. I can't thank you enough.

NADINE. James is great wow.
…
You two have a lot in common?

BETH. Martha.

NADINE. Fun to have a lot in common with your husband. Terrence and I have so little in common.

BETH. Great.

NADINE. Going back to the houses we were born in. His being small. Mine being huge. Mine just being so big.

BETH. Right.

NADINE. Nice wedding.

BETH. Thanks.

NADINE. Simple.

BETH. Yeah.

NADINE. You know, we had a whole little *area* in our house where girls who were dressed like you would sleep? And they'd take care of everything. In Worcester. And I became very close with a couple of them and I would always say: "Do you miss your family living here?"
And they'd smile and say: "You're our family, Nadine! *You're* our family!"

BETH. Ah.

NADINE. Different times back in Worcester.

BETH. …

NADINE. And Terrence, his family they had a *little* bit. But we got together at the wrong time of year. Not regular courting season like you, you Smart Smart Girl. And we were counting on corn but the bugs came. In the potatoes the bugs in the corn the bugs in the leaves the bugs in our BED. So our house just got smaller and smaller and further away 'til it was all the way over here. So life became simple.
There are bugs on me right now Beth, they're on my skin. Are you used to that?

BETH. …

NADINE. I just Can't get used to that. I'm getting used to that. You're getting used to that, *Nadine…* anyways Bugs yes and then, I learned that it was my job to—

BETH. Ah.

NADINE. *(Towards the chamber pot.)* Did you know it would be your job to—

BETH. Yes.

NADINE. Well I wanted to give this to you and make sure because—

BETH. Right.

NADINE. As of tomorrow—

BETH. I know Nadine, I know it's my job.

Beat.

NADINE. I'm sorry for getting you a Chamber pot… It says something funny on it… Read it outloud!

Beth doesn't know how to read.

BETH. Can you read it to me? My eyes are tired.

NADINE. *(Reading off the chamber pot.)* "Dear lovely wife pray rise and piss;
Take you that handle and I'll take this;
So let it be as they have said;
We'll laugh and piss and then to bed."

They do not laugh at all.

I could have sworn I laughed when I read that. I could have sworn I found it just funny.

BETH. *(Deeply disturbed, unamused.)* I find it funny.

NADINE. You do?

BETH. I do.

NADINE. Okay well good.

BETH. *(Not laughing.)* I think it's so funny.

NADINE. *(Not at all laughing.)* It's absolutely hilarious isn't it.

BETH. Yes.

*Mutual staring at chamber pot.
Nadine looks into the distance.*

NADINE. And would you look at *that*. Your sister is talking to my brother Thomas!

BETH. What?

NADINE. Your sister, *that* one. Is talking to my brother Thomas! (He's a printer but he broke his hand so he's staying with us for the winter)

BETH. She is huh.

NADINE. He never speaks to women.

BETH. Wow.

NADINE. But he's speaking to her. You know what that means!

BETH. I don't know about that.

NADINE. Can I say, Beth, since it seems like my brother is going to marry your sister, can I say:
Something Is Clearly Wrong In Your House.
We stitchers have been talking, and They. We. *I*. We. Hope You're All… Okay.

BETH. It was just a large winter of being in one room.

NADINE. Your father has big hands.

BETH. …

NADINE. Big knuckles.

BETH. …

NADINE. Must hurt.

Beth shuts down, rises to leave.

Don't forget your—

Nadine passes Beth her chamber pot.

Your Eyes, Oh wow, what is it I always say in this situation? Oh wow I love weddings because you get to say certain things and here's the thing I say when someone is crying. Like you.

BETH. I'm not.

NADINE. You are. A laughing bride makes a weeping wife. A weeping bride makes a laughing wife… I was a laughing bride.

Nadine gets so sad.

BETH. I'm going to find James.

> *Beth exits.*
> *Nadine exits.*
> *Bonnie and Abigail enter.*

ABIGAIL. I saw you eat a rock.

> *A guilty silence.*

You have to stop doing that.

BONNIE. I know.

> *They stare into the distance.*

ABIGAIL. That man is talking to Hannah. With the broken hand. What are they saying?

BONNIE. *(Staring ahead.)* "How'd you break your hand, Mister?"

ABIGAIL. "None of your business young lady."

BONNIE. "Tell me."

ABIGAIL. "A rock fell."

BONNIE. "Oh."

ABIGAIL. "From the sky. You have nice eyes."

BONNIE. "Thanks… You have big…ears."

ABIGAIL. "Thanks… Ears are so strange."

BONNIE. "They are."

ABIGAIL. "I have no idea what mine look like."

BONNIE. "Let me tell you."

ABIGAIL. I don't think this is what they're saying Bonnie.

> *Beth reappears, dressed for her new life. She has a coat and an overstuffed bag.*

BETH. She's gonna marry him.

ABIGAIL. What?

BONNIE. She's gonna marry him.

ABIGAIL. Looks like fun to meet strangers.

> *Abigail jumps back into the party. Bonnie follows.*
> *A beat.*
> *Harriet stands, breaking from her dead-person position.*

BETH. You're alive.

HARRIET. No I'm a ghost.

BETH. Did you see the wedding ghost?

HARRIET. You looked at me when you kissed him.

BETH. I thought I was looking at nothing.

HARRIET. No you were looking at Me you were looking at Ghost.

> *Staring.*
> *Then, all sisters enter, formally. They make a triangle.*
> *They nod to Beth, wishing her well.*
> *She exits through them.*

End of Part I

PART II

Bonnie, Hannah, Beatrice, and Harriet, singing, looking in the direction of Beth's exit.
Over the course of the song, day turns to dusk.

Sundial I

BONNIE, HANNAH, BEATRICE, and HARRIET.
Where did I fall from?
Was it a hayloft?
Was it much further away-ay-ay?

Oh Oh!
I don't know the time
Whoa-ho!
Build me a sundial
Oh Oh!

Hard on my ankles
Light on my forehead
I will try harder today-ay-ay

> *Beatrice is reading her book.*
> *Harriet is gutted, pacing, unwilling to surrender to the indoors.*
> *Bonnie is massaging her jaw.*
> *Hannah stands, nervous.*

HANNAH. Papa confirmed it. Thomas is coming over to bundle come nightfall. My very first bundling. I gotta go inside. I'm tardy. It's nightfall.

> *Beatrice and Bonnie sit, caught in the crossfire of Harriet and Hannah's confrontation.*

HARRIET. He ain't different just cuz he's a printer.

HANNAH. You don't know him.

HARRIET. You've spoken to him *once*.

HANNAH. Nice conversation though, Nicest of My Life, God Bless.

BONNIE. What'd he say?

HANNAH. It wasn't the words it was more the... Lord I'm nervous lord wow.

HARRIET. No one's different Hannah.

HANNAH. Some People Are and you know it.
...
We gotta go indoors, you know it.

HARRIET. I'm gonna puke.

HANNAH. Harriet.

HARRIET. Sleeping in that house with you bundling in the corner.

HANNAH. They're hangin' a curtain Mama says.

> *Instead of going indoors, Hannah sits with Beatrice and Bonnie.*
> *Beatrice reads, Bonnie surveys the sky.*

Gotta prepare for the bundling. I wish Beth was here, none of you know 'bout bundling. Wow I'm underprepared for bundling... Lord I do want to be bundling with Thomas but I...also want to wait... I want to wait a breath! Lord Please Stop Time!

HARRIET. Beatrice was reading a pamphlet she...read it's best to miss your first bundling. Makes for a better um. Breathes some fire into the loving so I think skip it didn't you read that Beatrice?

BEATRICE. *(Up from her book.)* One thing they don't tell you 'bout reading is you don't remember it very much.
(To Harriet, losing patience.) You know we gotta go in.

HARRIET. Papa knows you can't read a word so does Mama. You know what he says 'bout pretenders. So...
Better finish it fast, think about it.

> *Sisters mentally preparing for the atrocities of the indoors, not moving.*
> *Hannah is not quite getting up.*

HANNAH. Lord wow it's been nice out here.

> *Harriet pacing, desperate to keep them from going in.*
> *Bonnie staring straight ahead at the sky, back on the ground.*

BONNIE. *(A revelation.)* I think the sky is a wall.

HANNAH. I think it's more of a ceiling.

BONNIE. It's a Wall.

HANNAH. Thomas he's got these eyeballs they… It might be nice to bundle. Lord I'm shaky.

BEATRICE. Hannah you ain't breathing straight.

HARRIET. Can't go in 'til you breathe straight!

HANNAH. Let me just. Pray quietly for. Two hundred breaths. Be silent please.

The quiet of prayer. Harriet can't handle it.

HARRIET. Beatrice?

HANNAH. Sssshh.

HARRIET. Bonnie.

HANNAH. Sssshhh!

Harriet walks away from her sisters. She doesn't know what to do. She looks at the ground.

HARRIET. It'd be good if just someday. You could just. Pick up a thing. Like just this rock. And just. Speak into it. And someone very far away could like. Pick up a different thing and hear what you're saying. And speak back into their thing and just.

She picks up a rock, holds it to her face.

(Intimate.) Hi Beth.
I'm just thinking about you.
Yes.
Yes.
He what?
Okay well—
Okay.
Was just thinking 'bout you thought I'd give you a shout.
A shout?
Just a way of saying Hi like I'd shout at you like "BETH" "BETH" "BETH"

HANNAH. Be Quiet I'm Praying.

HARRIET. *(To Hannah.)* Hannah I'm talking to Beth.
(Back to the rock.) Sorry Beth.
…
Okay Quickly Then—How Is Doing The Thing With Him?
…
Oh. Huh.
Hannah's 'bout to bundle
Okay.
I said *okay*.
I said *okay fine we're going in*.
We're doing it.
We're walking back right now.
…
Yeah. We're all walking.

> *They aren't.*

Beth?

> *Nothing.*

(To Bonnie and Hannah.) She had to go wash her feet. Her feet are real tired.

> *Hannah finishes her prayer, which was made face-down into the dirt.*
> *Beatrice puts her book down beside Martha's gravestone rock.*

BONNIE. You finished the book?

BEATRICE. I did not like the ending.

> *Hannah stands. Bonnie stands. They are ready. Then: a loud rustling.*

HARRIET. GET DOWN! Something's coming.

> *Beatrice, Harriet, Hannah, and Bonnie on the ground, splayed low, like soldiers.*
> *Marcy storms in, in a huff, followed by Georgia. They don't pay any mind to the sisters.*

MARCY. A what?

GEORGIA. A Wet Nurse, I'm a—
MARCY. A what?
GEORGIA. A Wet Nurse?
MARCY. What?
GEORGIA. I take care of your baby so you don't have to.
MARCY. *(To Harriet on the ground.)* What is she talking about?
HARRIET. *(From the ground.)* Hi Marcy.
GEORGIA. Preacher and his wife hired me.
MARCY. Well you can go back to where you're living.
GEORGIA. Well there must be a mistake.
MARCY. I don't need help.
GEORGIA. But don't you want it?
MARCY. Preacher and Melinda Hired You?
GEORGIA. Yeah.
MARCY. How'd they find you?
GEORGIA. At a camp meeting.
MARCY. Oh.
GEORGIA. Round when the corn planted.
MARCY. Oh.
GEORGIA. Preacher was traveling, preaching.
MARCY. Right.
GEORGIA. For three days in a row and I got the jerks.
MARCY. Oh.
GEORGIA. God was right there inside me.
MARCY. He was.
GEORGIA. You know 'bout that?
MARCY. That's where your head pops off and you start grunting and barking?
GEORGIA. Yeah.
MARCY. And falling?

GEORGIA. And falling. I had the jerks like Preacher had never seen.

MARCY. Oh.

GEORGIA. I got them when he was preaching, so I think he felt a connection.

MARCY. Oh.

GEORGIA. He told me to confess Everything to him.

MARCY. And you did.

GEORGIA. I told him things. Things about… I don't want to get into those things I told him.

MARCY. …

GEORGIA. And he said "Let's Get You Out of Your House" Which was related to The Things I Told Him.

MARCY. Oh.

GEORGIA. *(Pleading.)* Don't make me go back there.

MARCY. What happened to *your* baby?

GEORGIA. S'God's business.

MARCY. I can care for my own baby.

GEORGIA. We can do it together?

MARCY. I want to be alone with my New Husband and Baby.

GEORGIA. Don't make me go back there.

MARCY. They think I'm incapable!

GEORGIA. But aren't you? On some level?… Don't make me go back there.

MARCY. I'm sorry!

> *Georgia grabs Marcy, pleading.*
> *Marcy shakes her off, running away.*
> *Georgia collapses, catatonic.*
> *Harriet jumps to Georgia.*
> *Hannah too.*

HANNAH. Dear Lord.

HARRIET. *Look* at her.

HANNAH. Is she okay?

HARRIET. Are You Okay?

GEORGIA. I don't wanna talk anymore.

HARRIET. You got somewhere to stay?

> *Georgia is silent.*

Stay here! It's great for sleep the air is good lie down!

> *Harriet elated—a reason to remain outdoors!*

(To sisters, suddenly energized.) She's got nowhere to stay. We gotta. We gotta care for this—what's your name?

GEORGIA. Georgia—

HARRIET. Gotta protect Georgia she—

HANNAH. But I gotta bundle!

HARRIET. God wants us helping sisters.

BONNIE. She ain't a sister.

HARRIET. God ain't noticing a difference.

HANNAH. Thomas is waiting.

HARRIET. *Go* Hannah, go in, start bundling look normal, but we gotta stay here she's got no one.
(To Georgia.) We got you, 'kay?

> *Harriet touches Georgia awkwardly, tries to hold her.*
> *Hannah begins to exit, Harriet shouts to her:*

Come back when he falls asleep! Twelve steps to the stump eighty steps to the—you know the way.

BEATRICE. She don't look well.

> *Georgia is silent. Harriet holds her like a baby.*
> *Georgia is uncomfortable.*

HARRIET. You don't have to say nothing just. Breathe through your nostrils think about flowers.

> *Noise from the woods.*

GEORGIA. What's that?

HARRIET. Porcupine. You're safe, we're here, we're gonna keep you warm.

BONNIE. She's lookin cold!

HARRIET. Gonna get her a blanket. Quiet your mind *Now*. Beatrice, read to her!

BEATRICE. But I finished the book!

HARRIET. Bonnie! Hold her.

>*Bonnie takes Harriet's position, holding Georgia like a baby.*
>*She hasn't touched a person basically ever.*
>*It's strange.*
>*Harriet runs to grab a blanket.*
>*Harriet returns with Martha's dress, drapes it across Georgia.*

BONNIE. That's not a blanket.

HARRIET. Couldn't find a blanket.

BONNIE. That's Martha's dress, Lord Help.

HARRIET. It's fabric, okay? It's just fabric.

>*Harriet hands Beatrice a book.*

Got this off Stephanie Doober's porch. *(Kneeling, looking at Georgia, who is attempting sleep.)* When I grabbed the fabric Hannah and the printer were lying real close. Bundling board between them. Wide awake you could hear them thinking. Mama and Papa were lying so far from eachother, Mama's face against the furthest wall.

BONNIE. *(Meaningfully.)* Furthest Wall.

HARRIET. Think before speaking to men, okay Abigail? Even one sentence can lead to a wedding.

BONNIE. Abigail's out.

HARRIET. You too Bonnie. Even one sentence.

>*Harriet looks at Beatrice. She commands:*

READ, *NOW*.

>*Beatrice stands. She opens the book. She doesn't know what to say. Then:*

BEATRICE. Now that it's night all the girls become dogs.
…
All their teeth turn to dog teeth. They run through the night. And then the sun rises and they turn back to girls. They stitch. But they're smiling. Because they know they will be dogs soon.
…
They finish dinner. The sun sets. They are dogs now. They run through the trees. Their tails are like. Are like. Are like moving so fast it's very. It's very hard not to watch.

BONNIE. *(Clutching tooth.)* Owwwwwwwwww.

HARRIET. Keep reading she likes the reading!

BEATRICE. *(Pacing with book.)* And then after many weeks this old magician says, "you gotta choose! Do you want to be a permanent dog? Or do you want to be a permanent girl?"
And they don't agree is the problem like three of them want to be dogs full time and three of them want to be girls full time and this one girl wants to be Both or Neither, she don't want to be a dog if she can't be a girl and she don't want to be a girl if she can't be a dog so—

From the woods, a grumbling.

GEORGIA. What's that?!

HARRIET. SSHHHHH you can sleep!

GEORGIA. Out here?

HARRIET. We're gonna find you a place indoors, but until we do we're out here.

Dennis enters.

DENNIS. Who's that?

BEATRICE. This is Georgia she—
We're caring for her 'til we find her a place!

Silence. He does not know what to say next. He does not want to leave.

DENNIS. Last year I saw your Ma on a horse.

BEATRICE. *(Confused.)* What?

DENNIS. She was on a horse and she was wearing your Papa's clothes. Was wearing his jacket and she'd drawn a fake beard on her face. Was crying.

HARRIET. We don't have a horse.

DENNIS. Was Ben Charney's Horse. Was trying to leave, go who knows where. Anyways. Always made me really love your Ma. Clever. Always made me real sad when I'd see her in her skirt in church after that.

HARRIET. She's not liking your presence, sorry Dennis it's not personal.

DENNIS. Bet she could stay with The Stembers.

BEATRICE. You think?

DENNIS. Mr. Stember's always doin favors. They're real Godly, they got space.

He begins to exit.

HARRIET. Dennis, bring another book.

DENNIS. Didn't know she could read.

HARRIET. Well she can.

He's gone.

Bonnie! Ask Mr. Stember if they got space ask nice talk quiet.

BONNIE. My tooth.

HARRIET. Your tooth ain't improving you gotta practice talking.

Bonnie runs, grabbing a rock for the road.

(To Georgia.) Now Now, turn your mind off.

> *Harriet clumsily plops Georgia onto the ground.*
> *Hannah waddles in, restricted by her bundling gear: an extremely tight nightgown with no armholes. Almost like a straightjacket. It should be difficult for her to move her arms, hands, and legs.*

You came!

HANNAH. I'm Still Bundling Just Sayin' Hi.

HARRIET. Check her temp'rature.

> *Hannah hops to Georgia in the middle of the field.*
> *She frees her hand from her bundling bag, placing it on Georgia's forehead.*
> *Harriet and Beatrice look on.*

HANNAH. I don't got a good sense for temperature.
…
When Mama wrapped me and Thomas. When she wedged the bundling board between us. She told this anecdote. Means fact. (Thomas says anecdote a lot.) She told one 'bout how she and Papa bundled. How she was weeping but he didn't notice. They were silent all night wrapped like mummies. She recommended talking. She said: "Hannah I Recommend Talking." So we talked! Thomas and I. He said I was *The Moon*, Lord Wow.

HARRIET. Talk quiet Georgia's sleeping.

GEORGIA. *(Eyes wide open.)* I can't sleep.

HARRIET. Grab leaves for her eyes. Keeps the starlight out.

HANNAH. What?

HARRIET. Trick from the Indians.

> *Hannah waddle-hops off, looking for leaves.*
> *Dennis enters.*

DENNIS. Here's a book.

BEATRICE. Thank you.

DENNIS. Wish I could stay but…………The Tavern.

> *He exits.*
> *Beatrice opens the book, standing.*

GEORGIA. *(Hopeful, sitting up.)* Is that a Bible?

HARRIET. No, but listen close.

> *Beat.*

BEATRICE. *(Staring hard at a page.)* There's a person
…
And she's living in this town with all these towers. She's living all

alone and she loves it.

Reads alone in a room by herself. She has friends, lots of different kinds of them.

And *once a week* she goes to a tiny room in one of the towers. And she sits in a chair facing *another person*. For less than a thousand breaths. Same Exact Time Each Week. And she says Whatever She Wants to this person. And this person gets paid to listen to her say Anything. She tells the stranger all the things she's not telling anyone else. She can say them however she wants to and the stranger won't tell anyone! The stranger doesn't know anyone she knows. And she never sees the stranger outside this little room. And it's not a stranger anymore… It's a person who knows her real well… Who she sees once a week for less than a thousand breaths.

HARRIET. *(Perplexed.)* And it's like…a job?

BEATRICE. Yeah it pays real decent.

> *Hannah enters with leaves.*
> *Harriet grabs them, places them over Georgia's eyes.*
> *Harriet, Beatrice, and Hannah lean over Georgia.*
> *They sing a sleep hymn.*

Wooden Chair

HARRIET, BEATRICE, and HANNAH.
If I tell myself
I am made for you
Will it make it so
We are meant to be?

Will I wake one day
In God's wooden chair?
Will we be the ones
Who are meant to be?

How Will I Know?
Chair, Make It So
When Will I Know?
Chair, Make It So

If I beg myself

If I bribe myself
Will I quiet down
For eternity?

Are we carved in stone?
Are we lost in sand?
Is this readable?
Or is it empty?

GEORGIA. *(More awake.)* It ain't workin'.

>*They failed.*

HANNAH. *(Looking in the direction of the house.)* Better go back. Don't want Thomas to wake see me gone... I'd like to bundle with him 'til we know every last thing about each other. How long's that gonna take?

>*Hannah hops away in her bundling bag, then a crazy idea hits her:*

If God would allow it, I'd like to bundle with Thirteen different people, not just Thomas.
Just lying with Multiple People for some breaths, that would show if he is different.
Takes different amounts of time to know different people I'm thinkin'.

>*She's gone.*
>*Abigail stumbles on, unsteady.*

ABIGAIL. Harriet!

HARRIET. *(Admonishing.)* Abigail where have you been there is *work* to do!

ABIGAIL. I pushed Henry in a wheelbarrow to a corn party! Had all this cider.

HARRIET. Henry?

ABIGAIL. You know...with...

HARRIET. With what?

ABIGAIL. The...

HARRIET. The what?

BEATRICE. *(She knows Henry.)* With the no legs.

HARRIET. Oh.

ABIGAIL. I'm drunk. From a corn party.

BEATRICE. How is it?

ABIGAIL. I like being drunk. I talked to a mailman. *(A warning.)* There's Gonna Be Mail *Everywhere.*

>   *Abigail sees Georgia, crumpled on the ground.*

Who's she?

HARRIET. This is Georgia she's got nobody. She doesn't wanna talk (which is *FINE* Georgia). Get her some water will you?

>   *Abigail tumbles down.*

ABIGAIL. Why is everything spinning?

BEATRICE. Oh Dear Lord.

HARRIET. Close your eyes.

ABIGAIL. Spinning faster!

BEATRICE. Lord Help.

HARRIET. She's gonna puke.

ABIGAIL. Everything is SPINNING.

HARRIET. *(To Beatrice.)* Get her some water

>   *Beatrice exits.*
>   *Bonnie enters.*

BONNIE. She can stay with Stembers once their corn comes. Mr. Stember said God Bless!

HARRIET. She can?!

BONNIE. Got farmhands staying 'til their corn comes but then they got space!

HARRIET. *(To Georgia.)* Georgia did you hear that? You don't gotta go nowhere! You just stay out here a little longer countin' stars. Then you got a Nice place indoors.

GEORGIA. Oh Lord, When?

HARRIET. When their corn comes, anyday now—Stembers they're real gentle. Real peaceful over there.

GEORGIA. *(Sitting up, elated.)* God Bless!

HARRIET. *(Slamming Georgia down.)* Now let yourself sleep, sleep's a choice.

> *The crunch of Bonnie eating a rock.*
> *Then, excruciating pain.*
> *It's an infirmary on the ground with drunk Abigail, traumatized Georgia, Bonnie's dental situation.*

BONNIE. OWWWWWWWW—

HARRIET. Bonnie.

BONNIE. OWWWWWW.

> *Harriet tries to comfort Bonnie, but touching is not her strength.*

HARRIET. *(To Georgia.)* I'd pull her tooth myself but then she'd hate me so… Gotta find a stranger for some things.

> *Beatrice enters with a heavy pail of water, spilling over.*
> *Sisters lounging on the ground, things are looking up.*

BEATRICE. Here's water!

HARRIET. *(To Georgia.)* Drink!

BEATRICE. Got this book, from Church!

HARRIET. Great, Read!

BEATRICE. This one I'm reading to myself.

BONNIE. *(Scanning surroundings.)* Oh My God. What if there was just a house…with walls that went up to the sky. And a thousand levels!

HARRIET. How you gonna get to the top?

BONNIE. Stairs?

HARRIET. Think of how many breaths it would take to walk to the sky on *stairs*, Bonnie.

BONNIE. Oh My God. You'd make a smaller box with walls. And

with a floor and ceiling, and you'd put that box inside. Hook that box to a rope. And *someone* could pull you all the way up and all the way down, you know?

HARRIET. You're just talkin' 'bout towers.

BONNIE. But with a box inside that moves you to the top!

ABIGAIL. Who's gonna pull that rope?

HARRIET. Seems like a bad job.

> *Sisters try to sleep.*
> *Dennis enters, carrying the gigantic barrel. He is quietly traumatized.*

DENNIS. *(To Beatrice.)* On my way to the tavern.

> *Beatrice is reading. The rest are stargazing, spacing out.*

Busy night.

> *The quiet of hoping for conversation.*

The Hanging.

> *Beat.*

You know my dad he really relies on hangings? When they canceled that Hanging in May. The Bald Rapist. When The Bald Rapist killed *himself* a few days before the public event. Lost a lotta business in The Tavern... So now, the Tavern Guys. Us bartenders. My brothers and I. We monitor the men they're hanging, sit with 'em all day, make sure they're stayin' alive for the event.
...
I've been staring at this guy *all* day. He's been looking right back at me and I wish I didn't know what he did.
(To Beatrice.) What are you reading?

BEATRICE. About men.

DENNIS. What about them?

BEATRICE. How they're always explaining things.

DENNIS. Oh.

BEATRICE. How they assume people are interested in what they're speaking?

DENNIS. Oh.

BEATRICE. Whereas I assume no one's interested so I don't speak nothing.

DENNIS. I'm interested.

BEATRICE. In what.

DENNIS. In what you're—

Harriet perks up.

HARRIET. It's not courting season, Dennis.

DENNIS. It actually is? I'm not. But. It is.

HARRIET. Dennis you ever pulled a tooth?

DENNIS. *(He hasn't.)* I don't know.

HARRIET. You don't *know*?

DENNIS. No.

HARRIET. Well—

DENNIS. Can I lie down?

HARRIET. Not unless you. Put on a dress and knew how to. Pull a tooth, then you could lie down for… Sixty breaths. But at the end of those sixty breaths, you gotta pull Bonnie's tooth, so…
Think about it.

He doesn't want to go, but is not currently able to commit to pulling a tooth.

DENNIS. Think you're real fun to talk to. Both of you.

HARRIET. We ain't talking.

DENNIS. Yeah so…so when we do I notice it more?

The quiet of hoping for conversation.

Off I go.

*Dennis exits.
Night keeps falling.
Harriet picks up a rock.
Holds it to her head.*

HARRIET. Hi Beth......Yeah. Oh I got time. Just talk quiet. Uh huh. Uh huh.

> *Sisters all sleep.*
> *And sleep and sleep.*
> *Then: red light pours over them, flickering.*
> *The sound of a fire.*
> *Abigail wakes, sees something awful.*

ABIGAIL. Look!

> *The rest wake, stand, staring into distant flames.*

BEATRICE. Oh no.

BONNIE. Lord Help.

HARRIET. Oh no.

ABIGAIL. It's—

HARRIET. My Word.

ABIGAIL. It's the Stembers!

GEORGIA. Lord Help.

BONNIE. There's Rhonda Stember.

ABIGAIL. There's Wendy Stember.

HARRIET. But I don't see most Stembers.

BEATRICE. Just Wendy and Rhonda.

BONNIE. Papa's out there, putting it out.

ABIGAIL. They're out of water.

HARRIET. They're peeing on it.

BEATRICE. Ten men peeing on that fire.

> *Dennis returns, ashen.*

DENNIS. They were Good Honest folks.

> *Georgia knows what this means: no hope for her indoors.*
> *She is on the verge of tears.*

GEORGIA. I'm going.

HARRIET. NO! Sleep here.

GEORGIA. I can't.

HARRIET. You were!

GEORGIA. Was closing my eyes but I can't with the… I gotta be alone… I gotta sleep alone… I gotta be going.

HARRIET. But—

GEORGIA. Thank you.

> *Georgia exits.*
> *They stare into the fire, amazed.*

ABIGAIL. I just think it'll be nice when more things are made of metal.

BEATRICE. I think it'll be nice to be able to go through the sky on the way to different places.

ABIGAIL. I think it'll be stressful we don't know how the sky is.

BONNIE. I just think it'll be nice when the indoors and the outdoors are a little more separated.

ABIGAIL. I think it would be nice if you could pay a few cents every month somewhere. Just in case everything you owned burned. And if everyone just paid a few cents every month to somewhere. Then that money could be used to replace all of the things that burned.

HARRIET. Wouldn't fix people but it could help with the things.

/ / /

> *Dusk, days later.*
> *Hannah stands.*

HANNAH. I killed the cow!

HARRIET.	BONNIE.	BEATRICE.
Oh no!	Oh Lord.	Oh Hannah!

HANNAH. Papa's in a rage, says I can't be bundling that's the punishment. Mama says too many stomachs to fill without the cow so… better move forward with the courting, get married.

HARRIET. Oh Hell.

> *Beat.*

BEATRICE. *(Sensitive.)* Potato?

Hannah nods.

HARRIET. Oh Hell!

HANNAH. I didn't mean to!

ABIGAIL. *(To Harriet.)* People drop potatoes!

HANNAH. Lord Help.

ABIGAIL. Cows choke!

HANNAH. But I Dropped The Potato That Our Cow Choked On. …
Papa says we all gotta come inside. Mama says All must be courting by Tuesday, or you're gonna need to earn real wages.
Someone's going to New Jersey. There's some rich folks in New Jersey looking for a girl. Take care of babies in New Jersey. Someone's doing that Mama says.

ABIGAIL. I can't cuz I'm youngest.

HARRIET. I can't cuz I—

Harriet begins coughing uncontrollably.

BEATRICE. I s'pose I could.

BONNIE. S'pose I could too.

HARRIET. No One Is Going To New Jersey!

Hannah starts to go inside.

HANNAH. The Lord is Funny Sometimes.

HARRIET. If you go indoors you know you're stuck with him!

HANNAH. Thomas is different I'm thinking.

Harriet grabs the nearest rock, speaks into it.

HARRIET. Beth! What's it like being married?… Oh It's like being pregnant? What's it like being pregnant?… Oh you're vomiting all the time, you feel really really really sick, you feel very very Alone. Okay, just wanted to check—Hannah was wondrin'!

HANNAH. I've *got to* Harriet.

HARRIET. We can go to the woods!

HANNAH. No we / can't.

> *Harriet tumbles over, coughing and hyperventilating.*

HARRIET. I. Can't. Breathe. Oh My God.

ABIGAIL. She's coughing.

BONNIE. Oh no!

HARRIET. *(To Hannah.)* Do Not Go.

BONNIE. Oh nooo!

ABIGAIL. Oh no. Oh no no no.

> *As she convulses, Harriet moves towards the perimeter.*

HARRIET. *(Through very extreme coughing.)* Going
To
Those
Woods
Over
Yonder
Don't
Want
You
To
See
This.

> *Dramatically, Harriet collapses, motionless, on her way to the woods.*

/ / /

> *Golden daylight.*
> *Bonnie, Beatrice, and Abigail sing the wedding song.*
> *At the end of the song, they place a veil on Hannah's head.*

Wedding Song II

BONNIE, BEATRICE, and ABIGAIL.
Sing this
Upside down
In your
Darkest night

*In the
Morning light
Under
Piney trees
Please just
Sing this song
Don't ask
Why right now
It's your
Only task
Young bright
Future Bride
You will*

*You will be married today
You will be married today
You will be free to stop
Singing
Tomorrow
Stop
Singing
Tomorrow*

>*Sisters exit.*

Hannah's Wedding

>*Harriet "dead" on the ground.
>Nadine again, in her cupcakey dress.
>She gives Hannah a present. This time, it's in a box. Exactly the size of a chamber pot.*

NADINE. You can open it later.

HANNAH. Thanks.

NADINE. I hope you like it.

HANNAH. I'm sure I will.

NADINE. You killed your family's cow but now you get a whole new life *huh*? Now you're part of my family now you're sleeping next to my brother.

HANNAH. Yeah.

NADINE. My brother the printer.

HANNAH. Yes.

NADINE. *(Doesn't realize she is saying this out loud.)* I can't believe my brother the printer is marrying a gal who can't read.

HANNAH. …

NADINE. But don't think printing is easier than fieldwork! Fields have rhythms, printing is *nonstop*.

HANNAH. I know.

NADINE. In the winter his hands will bleed.

HANNAH. He told me.

NADINE. From the metal and the cold.

HANNAH. He told me.

NADINE. *(Sharp, eye contact.)* I like my brother a lot. Terrence my husband, he's not like my brother. He doesn't know me like my brother does… *I wish we could trade!*

HANNAH. You want to marry your brother?

NADINE. Don't you?

HANNAH. Don't have brothers.

NADINE. But you know what I mean.
(Staring into the party, horrified.) Is that your sister?

HANNAH. Yeah.

NADINE. Is she eating a rock?

HANNAH. …

NADINE. Oh Lord She's Eating A Rock.

HANNAH. I don't know why she does that.

NADINE. Oh My Lord.

HANNAH. She has to stop doing that.

   Bonnie enters, happy.

Hi Bonnie.

NADINE. Hello.

BONNIE. Hi.

NADINE. I'm going to go home now.

> *Leaving, Nadine leans over to Bonnie.*

(A harsh whisper.) You should really see a doctor

> *Nadine is gone.*
> *Hannah follows, returning to her wedding party.*
> *Beatrice appears.*
> *Bonnie and Beatrice look at the party.*

BEATRICE. Look at Abigail pushing Neighbor Henry in that wheelbarrow.

BONNIE. They're "dancing."

BEATRICE. That's a funny-looking dance.

BONNIE. They kiss.

BEATRICE. What?

BONNIE. They Kiss!

BEATRICE. But… He has no legs.

BONNIE. Don't need legs to kiss.

> *Harriet stands from her dead-pose, twigs in her hair and dirt on her face.*

HARRIET. Why is Abigail pushing him how's that *her* job?

BEATRICE. They're dancing.

> *They watch Abigail and Henry "dance."*

HARRIET. Papa wouldn't let her marry a man with no legs…… would he?

BEATRICE. I don't know. I think it would make him discomfortable but—

> *Abigail appears, beaming.*

HARRIET. Abigail! Why are you shaking that poor boy in that wheelbarrow?

ABIGAIL. We're dancing. And you know him. And his name is Henry. And he is Good. And he says he's got a feeling in his stomach.

BONNIE. What?

ABIGAIL. A feeling! In his stomach! About God making us for each other. Making us on purpose for each other.

HARRIET. A feeling about God in his *stomach*…?

ABIGAIL. And I've got a feeling in my stomach, too. Not about God doing it on purpose but about like… When I say his name my stomach like. Makes this little doooop. You ever had that feeling in your stomach round one person's name Beatrice?

BEATRICE. No.

ABIGAIL. Bonnie?

> *Bonnie has not.*

HARRIET. But if *your* legs ever get removed how's that gonna work? How's he gonna push *you* around?

> *Hannah appears, dressed for her new life.*
> *A coat, an overstuffed bag, armfuls of books.*

HANNAH. Thomas' printer friends gave me these books. You can have them, Beatrice.

> *Beatrice takes them.*

BEATRICE. Bonnie, wanna take one to New Jersey?

HARRIET. *(Alarm.)* New Jersey?

BONNIE. *(Somber.)* Papa confirmed it. Says it makes logic.

BEATRICE. *(Somber.)* They're gonna pull her tooth in New Jersey.

> *Bonnie, Beatrice, Abigail, and Harriet look to Hannah.*
> *Formally, they make a triangle.*
> *They nod to Hannah, seeing her off.*
> *She exits through them.*

End of Part II

PART III

This time, Harriet does not sing.
She is looking off in the direction of Hannah's exit.
Abigail, Bonnie, and Beatrice sing.

Sundial Part II

ABIGAIL, BONNIE, and BEATRICE.
Master of crickets
Insects of Worcester
Pray give me something to say-ay-ay

Oh Oh!
I don't know the time
Whoa-ho!
Build me a sundial
Oh Oh!

Freeze in the cellar
Joy spins a cobweb
Why is the black sky so gray-ay-ay?
Why is the black sky so gray-ay-ay?
Why is the black sky so gray-ay-ay?

/ / /

> *Deep night.*
> *Dennis in Martha's dress, on the ground.*
> *He looks like a sister.*
> *Harriet stands above, strong.*
> *Bonnie lies in pain.*
> *Beatrice reads.*

HARRIET. Sixty breaths are up Dennis.

DENNIS. Give me... Four hundred more.

HARRIET. We said sixty. After sixty you'd pull the tooth and be on your way.

DENNIS. On my way *to what*?

> *Abigail appears, beaming.*

ABIGAIL. Papa confirmed it.
I can marry Henry although he doesn't advise it. Papa says he'd rather I marry someone with legs. Mama says Henry's got caring features. Papa says if Henry can support us I can dig my own grave and lie in it!

HARRIET. *(Suddenly.)* I see a bear!

BEATRICE. What?

HARRIET. There's a BEAR!

> *Harriet successfully scares them into a tight clump in the center of the dirt.*
> *Bonnie has a revelation:*

BONNIE. I Just Realized. You could make a house with no walls just ceilings. With walls that are clear!

ABIGAIL. You mean windows?

BONNIE. Could see animals and trees but they wouldn't come in!

> *Abigail looks above, a revelation of her own:*

ABIGAIL. I think it would be nice if there was a way for someone to. Watch us. Not someone who knows us. Not someone who's nearby. But someone who's like… Looking at a small box with little versions of us on it? Like little drawings of us that that move when we move!
Seeing the view from up tall. Making sure we're okay. And we never see the person and we never meet the person. But the person is there, watching, making sure we're okay.

BEATRICE. You're talkin' 'bout God.

HARRIET. Not God she means just a Good Person who is just Awake at night getting Paid or something to look at a box with us on it.

> *In the corner we hear rustling.*
> *It's Georgia. Covered in dirt.*

Georgia is that you?

BONNIE. Hi Georgia!

> *With caution, sisters approach.*

ABIGAIL. Where did you go?

GEORGIA. Nowhere.

BEATRICE. Did you go home?

GEORGIA. No.

> *Georgia is timid.*
> *Beatrice takes her hand, bringing Georgia to the center of the dirt.*
> *The rest back off, spectating.*

BEATRICE. Why can't you go home, Georgia?

…

GEORGIA. You want me to say things about what they'd.
About when my father.
How my brothers.

…

How my mother. Stopped. Making expressions on her face. And I don't. This isn't the night where I say those things.

> *They kneel, facing each other.*

BEATRICE. You can tell us Georgia…
Pretend you're in a tower. Alone with a stranger. Who doesn't know anyone you know. Whose job is to really focus on everything you say. To make eye contact and ask basic questions until you say everything out loud.

> *Beatrice becomes a therapist.*
> *The others slowly maneuver to get a clear view of Georgia's face as she speaks.*

GEORGIA. They…
My dad my brothers…
I was—
I can't. I won't.

…

But I have killed I don't know how many bugs since they…
I started just Killing bugs after they…
I kept count. Ten dead bugs. Hundred dead bugs. Nine hundred. And then I reached a number. Nine hundred and ninety-nine thousand. And I didn't know what was next.

What is after that?

…

My youngest brother, he didn't. Nothing. He was so good. He watched the others.

…

He'd sleep next to me. Keep me guarded. Oh, I miss him!
But you can't sleep on Two Sides of a person is a frustrating thing I've found. You gotta pick one side. He picked left.

> *The others are rapt, devastated, concerned.*

HARRIET. Where will you go now?

DENNIS. Yeah.

GEORGIA. *(Terrified.)* Is that a boy—

BEATRICE. Yes but he's—

GEORGIA. *(Disaster.)* I said All That to a—

DENNIS. It's okay.

BEATRICE. It's okay!

ABIGAIL. It's okay.

DENNIS. It's okay.

HARRIET. It is!

> *Georgia is ready to run.*

BEATRICE. Come sit.

> *Georgia is gone.*
> *Harriet is furious.*
> *She turns to Dennis.*

HARRIET. Pull her tooth before I get your brothers.

> *But he still doesn't know how to pull a tooth.*

Dennis we said *sixty* breaths. This was the deal.

> *Dennis grabs the pail of water, Bonnie's hand.*
> *He kneels in front of her, as Beatrice did with Georgia seconds ago.*
> *The others back off, spectating from afar.*

He dips his hand in the water, opens Bonnie's mouth.

DENNIS. *(Doctor small talk.)* New Jersey huh?

ABIGAIL. Will you live in a mansion?

BONNIE. The walls are real tall.

HARRIET. If we pull the tooth here she can stay here!

BONNIE. *(To Harriet, leveling.)* I gotta sleep far from rocks. I start thinking. And once I'm thinking 'bout it a clock starts. And it's like When. When. When. When. Rock. Rock. Rock. Rock. And I *know* I'm gonna eat one, only question is When.

ABIGAIL. You're gonna stop eating rocks. You're gonna come to my wedding.

> *Dennis sticks his finger into the back of Bonnie's mouth.*
> *It's long and terrible.*
> *She's squealing.*
> *A sudden jolt, her head is against the dirt.*
> *She seems hurt.*
> *There is blood.*
> *But, miraculously, Bonnie's squealing has turned to laughter.*
> *Her pain is gone.*
> *She has never felt better.*
> *Laughing hysterically, Bonnie embraces Dennis, toppling him.*

BONNIE. Thank you!

> *She stands, completely different than before.*

I'm goin' inside now, I gotta stop the bleeding.

HARRIET. Bonnie.

BONNIE. *(Harsh, honest.)* I've got to.

> *Bonnie takes a breath, preparing for her next life.*

BEATRICE. *(Reassuring Bonnie.)* I'm reading that in New Jersey people are real nice to strangers.

HARRIET. *(Threatening.)* I heard there's lots of mosquitoes in New Jersey.

BEATRICE. *(Reassuring.)* I'm reading that the eggs are DELICIOUS!

HARRIET. *(Threatening.)* I heard New Jersey is closed until winter!

BONNIE. *(Simple.)* I have to go Harriet.

A glimmer of acceptance.

HARRIET. I know.

BONNIE. Goodbye.

Bonnie leaves.

BEATRICE. I'm reading that the houses in New Jersey are like towers!

Sisters watch her go.

///

The deep of night.
Everyone sleeps, except Harriet, who picks up a rock.

HARRIET. Hello?
Beth—
Beth—
Can you hear me?
Beth?

It isn't working, she tosses the rock.

///

Even later.
Even Harriet sleeps.
Beatrice is reading one of Hannah's books.

DENNIS. *(Quietly.)* Beatrice?

BEATRICE. *(Quietly.)* I'm reading.

Silence.

DENNIS. *(Quietly.)* Isn't it dark?

Silence.

Beatrice?

BEATRICE. You know I'm trying to read every book ever written before I die, and I just realized that even if I read every breath I'm not working, every breath of the night, *still won't be able to finish them.* So... SHHHHH.

DENNIS. Here.

> *Dennis takes a candle from his bag.*
> *He tries to light it.*
> *It's too windy.*

BEATRICE. I can read in the dark.

DENNIS. Then read to me.

> *Beat.*

BEATRICE. You're right. It's a little dark. Wish I had a room to keep bright all night but...

DENNIS. You can use our shed! No one goes there.

BEATRICE. But then *you'd* come with me and I want to read *alone*.

DENNIS. *(Still wearing the dress.)* You could go alone. You could take the candle.
I ain't getting up.
I ain't taking this off.

BEATRICE. You're not trying anything?

DENNIS. I don't even know what to try... If you're gonna learn to read you gotta stare at those shapes a long time before it takes hold... Sixty steps to the brook then thirty steps to the barn then ninety steps to the shed.

> *Beatrice stands, takes the candle, heads towards Dennis' shed.*

///

> *A tad later.*
> *Dennis sleeping in a dress.*
> *Harriet sleeping in a dress.*
> *Abigail sleeping in a dress.*
>
> *Red light pours over them.*
> *The sound of a fire raging.*
> *Harriet wakes, sees something awful in the distance.*
> *They're looking in the direction of Beatrice's exit.*

HARRIET. Look!
ABIGAIL. What.
HARRIET. Look.
DENNIS. Oh—
ABIGAIL. Oh no.
DENNIS. Oh no!

> *Dennis runs to the fire, all the way offstage.*
> *Harriet and Abigail drop to their knees.*
> *They sing again, faster than before, wrecked and praying.*

Oh Abraham

HARRIET and ABIGAIL.
Oh Abraham
Do you need help?
Do you need time?
Can I ask you?

Oh Abraham
Am I off pitch?
Are you upstairs?
Am I outside?

I have to tell you my dream!
I was entirely green!
There were eight children!
Green green green!
I had no clue what to do!

Oh Abraham
Can you make sense?
Of all my dreams?
I need your help!

Oh Abraham
Butter is my work!
Stitching is nonstop!
Winter I am cold!

I have to tell you my dream!

I was entirely green!
There were eight children!
Green green green!
I had no clue what to do!

> *Dennis reappears, still wearing the dress, holding a bottle of alcohol.*
> *He passes out, drunk.*
> *Abigail sleeps.*
> *Only Harriet now.*

HARRIET.
That's my dream
Frightening dream
Oh Abraham
Oh Abraham
Oh Abraham

> / / /

> *Beth appears, very pregnant.*
> *Dennis, Abigail, and Harriet are strewn about the ground.*
> *Harriet sees Beth, hardly believing her eyes.*

HARRIET. *Beth.*

BETH. Hi Harriet.
Hi Abigail.

> Beat.

HARRIET. How's marriage?

BETH. It's so-so.

…

Did I miss the funeral? Horse lost control galloped into dark woods had to get off and calm her. Took a large time.

HARRIET. *Beth will you lie down?*

> *Harriet is desperate for Beth to join.*

Lie down Beth.

ABIGAIL. Yeah lie down.

BETH. *(Noticing Dennis in the dress.)* What's *that*? Lord Help! Is that Dennis? Are you two courting?

HARRIET. Let's lie down.

> *Beth doesn't think lying down is a good idea.*
> *She is very pregnant, she might never get back up.*
> *Harriet pleads.*

I can't tell you things. I can't write you things.

DENNIS. Say them to me I'll write them down.

HARRIET. Then I'll start relying on you.

BETH. What's wrong with that?

HARRIET. Not interested in relying on him.

…

DENNIS. I'm not courting.

BETH. Court! Why Not?

HARRIET. What you don't know and what he doesn't know is that I am just like this. Elderly man! From just Japan or just France and… I'm old and I'm wise so. When young men speak to me, I'm just confused like: Why are you speaking to this *man*?

BETH. That don't make logic.

DENNIS. I think it might.

HARRIET. Beth lie down.

> *Beth and Harriet both lie flat, face-up, with Dennis and Abigail.*
> *A four-pronged star.*
> *It's close to wonderful.*

BETH. Wow.

> *Marcy enters, sees them on the ground, notice's Beth's pregnant belly.*

MARCY. Beth?

BETH. *(From ground.)* Hi Marcy.

> *Beat.*

MARCY. *(Respectful.)* She was good.

ABIGAIL. Thank you Marcy.

> *Long silence.*

MARCY. One thing I admired about Beatrice was—

HARRIET. She couldn't read.

MARCY. I was going to say her needlework.

ABIGAIL. It's true.

MARCY. Great needlework.

> *Beth looks at Marcy from below.*

BETH. *(This is an important question.)* Is the baby keeping you up all night, Marcy?

MARCY. Everyone's asking that! Is The Baby Keeping You Up All Night?
And first it was just Hell Hell. That baby *Was* keeping me up all night. But recently. *We've* been waking the baby up. Francis and I. With our laughter. I didn't know he was funny. I didn't know *I* was funny. And we are so funny.
…
A couple months back I was just in a dark room with our baby.
Just wanting to be anything else. But then one morning I saw Francis.
When he didn't know I was awake, when he thought he was alone. And seeing him like that? Seeing him when he didn't know he was being seen.
…
I can't explain it

> *Marcy exits.*
> *Beth stands, abruptly; she doesn't look at Harriet.*

BETH. James and I are going West. More space I. Won't see people Anymore.
By people I mean You…
It's not that he's bad. It's just…

HARRIET. *(Quietly.)* I can deliver babies now.

BETH. *(Staring off, proud.)* Did you see my horse? Abigail *that's* my horse. Look at my horse.

> *Abigail stands, looks into the distance at Beth's handsome horse.*
> *Beth leaves.*
> *It is time.*
> *Dennis stands, begins exiting in his dress.*
> *Then, he stops:*

DENNIS. I want to be a mailman.

> *He's gone.*

/ / /

> *Later.*
> *Harriet's back is turned to Abigail.*
> *They are across the field from each other, in the middle of a confrontation.*

ABIGAIL. Don't be silent I just shared large news!

HARRIET. See how you feel about him in three years.

ABIGAIL. I *know* how I feel about him in three years. I know how I feel about him in *ten* years. There's permanent knowings!

HARRIET. So. When the ice comes, you'll be pushing Henry in a wheelbarrow round some city. And I'll be Dead.

ABIGAIL. Harriet!

HARRIET. Don't marry him.

> *Harriet runs to Abigail.*
> *She grabs her, tightly.*
> *It almost seems like a schmaltzy hug, but really it's Harriet preventing Abigail from moving or walking.*

ABIGAIL. But I decided.

HARRIET. Wait to decide.

ABIGAIL. But I wanted to decide something!

HARRIET. Decide to wait to decide!

> *Harriet's grip softens.*

They hold each other in the center of the dirt.
The following is muffled but clear, spoken into their embrace.

ABIGAIL. I think it'd be nice if there were more chairs with like. Very large wheels on both sides. I saw one in Worcester, Rich Man in it. Be nice if they had chairs like that for anyone.

HARRIET. I think it'd be nice someday, if everyone lived Alone and there were kitchens Everywhere.
So you could make these tiny little amounts of food, just for yourself, just when you're hungry anytime of the night.

They break apart, a burst of energy.
Abigail crouches down, illustrating on the dirt.

ABIGAIL. I think it'd be nice to like…carve tunnels underground? And build some trains inside them, so the trains don't hit animals! Cuz they're underground!

HARRIET. I think it'd be neat to like. Dance in a way that wasn't like. *With* someone and was just like. Lots of people dancing not really *with* anyone!

Abigail agrees!

I think it'd be good if people could do The Thing as much as they wanted without having babies.

ABIGAIL. I think it'd be fun to put large flat pieces of wood under your feet and like! Slide down a mountain when it *snows*!

HARRIET. Or tiny wheels under your shoes?

ABIGAIL. So your…your whole body is like a cart!

HARRIET. I think it'd be great if just… Instead of washing forks you could just throw them away after one meal, and buy big boxes full of them.

ABIGAIL. *(Scandalized, thrilled.)* That's a wasteful thought, Harriet.

A breath, they've found each other again.
They lie down looking at the sky.
A question burns.

What Is Heaven? I Know It's Not A Wheel.

HARRIET. It's just lying like this but against The Sky.

ABIGAIL. Ooh.

HARRIET. Martha she's lying like this against The Sky.

ABIGAIL. Huh.

HARRIET. So she saw Dennis wearing her dress. And Beatrice is to her right. And the babies are to her left. And George Washington too.

ABIGAIL. But if they're facing towards us, wouldn't they fall?

HARRIET. No… There's this force… Holding their backs hard to the sky…
You never stand up. And instead of seeing stars, you're seeing dirt you're seeing treetops. You're seeing horses and houses.

ABIGAIL. Seems worse than stars.

HARRIET. No! It looks mighty, from up far. Not the things themselves? But the movement kinda. Makes a pattern.
…
And when they drool, it *rains*.

> *The almost indecipherable sound of rain coming.*
> *They stare.*
> *A beat.*
> *Abigail sits up.*
> *She looks at Harriet.*
> *She has to go.*
> *She kisses her forehead.*
> *Stands.*
> *She's gone.*
> *Harriet is alone, back against the dirt.*
> *It's her worst nightmare, but also somehow different than she expected.*
> *The silence is long and difficult, she needs company.*
> *Quietly, she begins singing.*

Saddle

HARRIET.
Saddle below me
Reins in my hand

Hooves on the hilltop
Rocks on the land

Galloping onward
Trotting to sky
Why why why!
Oh tell me now—
Why why why!

> *Voices of unseen sisters gradually join from offstage, adding volume and harmony.*

Honey I call you
But you don't come
Sleeping in attics
Chewing your gum

Horsey oh will you
Survive the storm
Warm warm warm!
It's gonna get—
Warm warm warm!

> *Louder and louder, the fullest thing we've heard all night.*

Animal genius
Ya know me so well
Ya know my secrets
Ya cast your spell

Horsey oh will you
Take back the night
Light light light!

> *The voices cut, sharp.*
> *Harriet alone.*
> *She finishes, quietly.*

I promise you—
Light light light

> *Blackout.*

End of Play

PROPERTY LIST
(Use this space to create props lists for your production)

SOUND EFFECTS
(Use this space to create sound effects lists for your production)

Note on Songs/Recordings, Images, or Other Production Design Elements

Be advised that Dramatists Play Service, Inc., neither holds the rights to nor grants permission to use any songs, recordings, images, or other design elements mentioned in the play. It is the responsibility of the producing theater/organization to obtain permission of the copyright owner(s) for any such use. Additional royalty fees may apply for the right to use copyrighted materials.

For any songs/recordings, images, or other design elements mentioned in the play, works in the public domain may be substituted. It is the producing theater/organization's responsibility to ensure the substituted work is indeed in the public domain. Dramatists Play Service, Inc., cannot advise as to whether or not a song/arrangement/recording, image, or other design element is in the public domain.